TO

_____

FROM

_____

Bruce & Stan's Guide to God

Copyright © 1999 Bruce Bickel and Stan Jantz
Published by Garborg's
P. O. Box 20132, Bloomington, MN 55420

Design by Lecy Design

ISBN 1-58375-634-5

Even though millions of people before you have wondered about God, the search for Him is always a very personal thing. Everybody starts in a different place and goes about it in a different way.

JANUARY 1

We hope you have increased your reverence for God. He is not just a Big Guy in the Sky. He is the Almighty Creator of the Universe who, despite His awesome magnitude, wants to have an intimate relationship with each of us.

DECEMBER 31

Here's what **God** has promised you about your search for **Him:** *I know the plans I have for you...plans to prosper you and not to harm you, plans to give you hope and a future.... You will seek me and find me when you seek me with all your heart. I will be found by you* (Jeremiah 29:11-13).

JANUARY 2

The further you travel with God, the more you value and trust in His free (but priceless) and unfailing grace. (Remember, "grace" is God's undeserved favor or kindness.) With this gratitude for grace comes humility.

BIG IDEA

Without a doubt, the single most useful source of information for discovering, understanding, and knowing God is the Bible.

Jesus has promised to return to earth. Someday—and many Bible scholars believe it will be soon—Christ will return to earth. This time, He won't appear as a cooing baby but as a triumphant king.

DECEMBER 29

Jesus lived a human but perfect life. Jesus never committed a sin. He never had to say that He was sorry. He never had to ask God or anyone else for forgiveness. Paul said it simply: *He had no sin* (2 Corinthians 5:21).

JANUARY 4

Jesus said that when He comes again, "All the nations will be gathered before him: for a time of final judgment" (Matthew 25:32). Paul also wrote: *We must all appear before the judgment seat of Christ, that each one may receive what is due him for the things done while in the body, whether good or bad* (2 Corinthians 5:10).

DECEMBER 28

Our buried assumptions about God don't help us much in real life. What we "know" isn't enough. We feel compelled to search for the truth.

At the name of Jesus every knee should bow, in heaven and on earth and under the earth, and every tongue confess that Jesus Christ is Lord, to the glory of God the Father.

PHILIPPIANS 2:10-11

DECEMBER 27

In **Old Testament** times, God's presence was sometimes described as a powerful, shining light in the temple. After the coming of the Holy Spirit, God's place of residence changed. Here's Paul's amazing statement to **new believers:** *Don't you know that you yourselves are God's temple and that God's Spirit lives in you?* (1 Corinthians 3:16). This is the "indwelling" of the Holy Spirit. It applies to every believer.

JANUARY 6

In the Old Testament, God was present only with particular people and in particular places. In the Gospels, God was present in bodily form in Jesus. Today, God is present in a third, most amazing way. Through the Holy Spirit, He lives inside all who believe. Now He is Immanuel ("God with us") always!

DECEMBER 26

The Bible teaches that spirit beings are either good or evil now, but were all originally created as angels. When Satan rebelled against God, many of the angels followed him. That ill-fated power play began the universal distinctions of good and evil, holiness contrasted with sin, God versus Satan.

JANUARY 7

For in Christ all the fullness of the Deity lives in bodily form.

COLOSSIANS 2:9

DECEMBER 25

After observing the incredibly complex and diverse nature of the universe and the living things on planet earth, it's reasonable to conclude that it was all brought into being by an all-powerful, caring Creator who is personally interested in His creation.

Predictions in the Old Testament about this Messiah were many and specific. These predictions are referred to as "prophecies" because "prophets" were the ones who announced them. All gave clues as to how the Messiah could be identified: where and when He would be born, His family tree, when and how He would die, and more.

DECEMBER 24

Often what we're looking for isn't what we end up with, or what we really need. In your explorations about God, our personal encouragement to you is to leave yourself open to something bigger than you've ever imagined or thought possible.

JANUARY 9

The man, Jesus Christ, said that He was the long-awaited Messiah. He fulfilled each prediction made about the Messiah, and lives a life to prove He was, in fact, who He claimed to be.

DECEMBER 23

For it is by grace you have been saved, through faith—and this is not from yourselves, it is the gift of God—not by works, so that no one can boast.

EPHESIANS 2:8-9

JANUARY 10

All throughout the Old Testament, God promised the Jews that He would send a king who would establish God's kingdom on earth. This "deliverer" was referred to as the Messiah. He would be God coming down to earth.

DECEMBER 22

"There will always be the seeming contradiction—that while God's saving grace is always and forever free, it is never, never cheap."

HERMAN W. GOCKEL

JANUARY 11

"The Eternal being, who knows everything and who created the world universe, became not only a man but (before that) a baby, and before that a fetus inside a woman's body. If you want to get the hang of it, think how you would like to become a slug or a crab."

C. S. LEWIS

DECEMBER 21

God loves His creation, especially those special creatures He made in His image. He desires nothing greater than to have us glorify Him in all we do, and to truly enjoy everything about Him.

JANUARY 12

How does God speak to you? Well, remember that the Holy Spirit is living inside you and can bring the comfort and wisdom of God to your thinking, often through the Bible.

DECEMBER 20

And there's more good news: The very Spirit of God is alive in us to help us do what seems impossible—every day. We will attain that Christlike mark one day—when we are united with Christ in heaven.

JANUARY 13

Jesus was born of a virgin. You could call this fact "inconceivable," but the Bible tells us that Mary was a virgin when she became pregnant with Jesus. In a nonsexual way, she became pregnant by the Holy Spirit. Thus, Christ had parentage which was both human and divine. The theological word for this event is *incarnation,* meaning God took on a human form.

DECEMBER 19

"Deity indwelling men! That is Christianity, and no man has truly experienced the power of Christian belief until he has known this for himself as a living reality."

A. W. TOZER

JANUARY 14

BRUCE & STAN SAY

We've found that the traveling through the unknowns of life is easier—and at times even exciting—when you're following the One who knows exactly where every road leads.

DECEMBER 18

God's idea of a perfect world was a place where a man and woman could enjoy perfect happiness in perfect freedom, including the freedom to choose—even to choose against God.

JANUARY 15

God is a spirit. Yet God has a personality. So why should it be different with the Holy Spirit? Jesus referred to the Holy Spirit as "He" many times, including this incredible passage in the Gospel of John, where Jesus promises the Holy Spirit to His disciples: *I will ask the Father, and he will give you another Counselor to be with you forever—the Spirit of truth. The world cannot accept him, because it neither sees him nor knows him. But you know him, for he lives with you and will be in you* (John 14:16-17).

DECEMBER 17

BRUCE & STAN SAY

Pleasing God is a good description of the opposite of sin. Pleasing God is what we were created for and originally intended to do.

Jesus the Son Is God. Unlike other founders of major world religions—Buddha, Confucius, Mohammed come to mind—who are known primarily for what they *said,* Jesus is known primarily for who He *was.* Jesus is central to Christianity, which consequently must stand or fall based on whether or not He was God.

DECEMBER 16

Jesus frequently spoke in *parables*—using a common object or experience from daily life to illustrate a spiritual truth. For example, He used the story of a farmer planting seeds in four types of soil—roadside, rocky, weed-infested, and fertile—to illustrate how different people respond to God's message of new life.

JANUARY 17

You can't skip "the faith step" (and neither can anyone else). Many things can be proved scientifically. But God isn't one of them. In fact, the Bible says, *Without faith it is impossible to please God, because anyone who comes to him must believe that he exists and that he rewards those who earnestly seek him* (Hebrews 11:6).

DECEMBER 15

Why did God create man, especially since He must have known how man would respond to His command to obey Him? And why does He put up with us now? The "Why are we here?" question got its best-known answer in the Westminster Confession (a church creed from 1646): *The chief end of man is to glorify God and enjoy Him forever.*

JANUARY 18

See then that ye walk circumspectly, not as fools, but as wise (Ephesians 5:15 KJV). *Circumspectly* in this verse means "mindful of consequences." We're not talking about the difference between great consequences and okay consequences, either. What you "step in" can be a land mine that blows up your life! The apostle Paul liked to drive this point home.

DECEMBER 14

The Holy Spirit spoke eternal truth through writers and prophets. The Holy Spirit brought God's message to the men who spoke for God (prophets), and those who wrote the text of the Bible.

JANUARY 19

The fruit itself is relatively unimportant. Adam and Eve's great offense was the act of deliberate disobedience. In fact, the only rule God imposed was to refrain from eating the fruit of one tree; all the other produce in the Garden was available to Adam and Eve. Compliance with God's single command should have been pretty easy, and this makes the act of disobedience all the more offensive.

DECEMBER 13

Webster's Dictionary says that to *inspire* means "to breathe or blow into." Inspiration is defined as "a divine influence." *You can trust the Bible completely.* Because God inspired the writers through the Holy Spirit, He controlled the process. He "breathed in" what He wanted. Nothing more, nothing less. That's why we can trust what we read.

JANUARY 20

Worship is a natural expression of appreciation to God for who He is and His great gift of salvation. True worship is expressed not only in words but also in actions.

DECEMBER 12

KEY VERSE

All Scripture is God-breathed and is useful for teaching, rebuking, correcting, and training in righteousness so that the man of God may be thoroughly equipped for every good work.

2 TIMOTHY 3:16-17

JANUARY 21

If God is for us, who can be against us?... No, in all these things we are more than conquerors through him who loved us.

ROMANS 8:31,37

DECEMBER 11

We aren't instructed to fly through the Christian life; we aren't told to dash or even jog. It's a walk—slow, steady, deliberate, and doable. If God had wanted something more flamboyant and drastic, He could have arranged it.

JANUARY 22

Even though God is beyond our complete understanding, we don't need to stay in a fog about Him. Or be stuck with a small or silly concept of God. Or carve an idol to worship. The Bible gives a definite picture of a multifaceted God. He is an invisible reality, yet He has characteristics of a person: He knows; He hears; He feels; He speaks.

DECEMBER 10

Setting aside time each day for Bible reading and prayer is often called "having daily devotions" or "taking a quiet time." Is it a must? Nope. On the other hand, we recommend you think of it as daily food. You don't have to read the Bible daily. You don't have to eat food daily either. But if you want to thrive, regular eating makes a lot of sense.

BRUCE & STAN SAY

JANUARY 23

The Holy Spirit, working from the inside, produces an outward effect. As the maturity continues, the Christian starts to act more and more like Christ.

Jesus Christ was *not* simply God wearing a human disguise—like Superman putting on his "Clark Kent" glasses—so no one would recognize Him. At the same time, Jesus Christ was *not* just a human being who occasionally got a dose of supernatural powers—like Popeye after eating his spinach—so He could get people's attention.

The fact that life is sustained in just one place in the entire universe has always given us a greater appreciation for the God who made us. From the first day of Creation to the last, from the smallest molecules to the largest stars, God made everything so that life would be possible on planet earth. You and I aren't lost in space. And we're not a freak biological accident. We're the focus of God's creative power and perfect love.

BRUCE & STAN SAY

DECEMBER 8

God is Omniscient.

God knows everything. All things past, all things future. He knows all things technical (like the chemical composition of DNA) and all things trivial (like the number of hairs on your head). He knows you better than you know yourself.

JANUARY 25

Once you harness your energy, you start moving closer to where you want to go. Maturity isn't just soaked up; you learn and grow day by day. It's a process. Time is your friend.

DECEMBER 7

Is your God stuck in a box?

Think about it for a moment: What is your image of God?... Limited notions about God work like the idols, or false gods—they may be limited, but at least they're convenient. Often a "god in a box" is the result of ignorance or fear.

JANUARY 26

The greatest tactical ploy of Satan and his demons is to keep us uninformed and naive about their existence. They want us to think that they don't exist, or that they are merely symbols of mischieviousness, or that they are confined to hell.

DECEMBER 6

God didn't create the heavens and the earth just for something to do. Or even so He could have it all to Himself. He made everything in perfect balance and harmony so that we could live here on earth and enjoy Him.

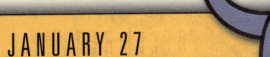

JANUARY 27

The Bible records thousands of prophecies concerning nations, cities, national and world leaders, and the coming of Jesus Christ. Nearly every fulfilled prophecy recorded in the Bible can be verified by historical records outside the Bible—and not one prophecy has been proven wrong.

DECEMBER 5

Before Jesus returned to heaven, He promised that "the Spirit of truth" would come. The disciples spent an intensive three-year training program with Jesus. Imagine how abandoned they felt when He told them He was leaving. But Jesus promised to send the Holy Spirit to fill their lives in a new way.

JANUARY 28

Since we're both proud dads, it helps us to think of God's love as being like parental love—it's made up of both affection and discipline. Mothers and fathers who display affection to a child without regard to discipline are not good parents (Okay, maybe they're good grandparents!). A parent who really loves a child expresses both tenderness *and* limits.

DECEMBER 4

"The Bible: There exists no document from the ancient world witnessed by so excellent a set of textual and historical testimonies and offering so superb an array of historical data on which an intelligent decision may be made. An honest [person] cannot dismiss a source of this kind. Skepticism regarding the historical credentials of Christianity is based upon an irrational bias."

DR. CLARK PINNOCK

JANUARY 29

God. A New Testament term, *theos,* meaning "the one true God." He is unique; He is the Creator; and He is the Savior.

DECEMBER 3

BIG IDEA

The good news is that God's message is always one of hope and welcome. Here it is, beautifully expressed in the most famous verse in the Bible. You might know it by heart: *For God so loved the world that he gave his one and only Son, that whoever believes in him shall not perish but have eternal life* (John 3:16).

JANUARY 30

GLAD YOU ASKED

So what's the deal? Are we set free from sin or not?

Romans 6:18 tells us that we are no longer *slaves* to sin. We have power and freedom to choose right living that we didn't have before. We're not in a losing war—even when some battles go badly.

DECEMBER 2

If you're still in the process of discovery, keep pointing your spiritual flashlight at the facts. Keep following the trail of evidence. At least you know now that God has made it possible for you to get through to Him.

As we try to grow in Christ, at times it will feel like we've moved two steps forward, one step back. Although the Christian has a new nature that wants to walk in obedience, his old nature, as it were, forgot to leave. You may agree with the apostle Paul: *For I have the desire to do what is good, but I cannot carry it out. For what I do is not the good I want to do; no, the evil I do not want to do—this I keep on doing* (Romans 7:18-19).

DECEMBER 1

Understanding that God created man *in His image* is critical. That we are made in God's image explains why every person who has ever lived has thought about God. God's image—His imprint—is there. It is this divine imprint which ultimately gives us our value.

FEBRUARY 1

And I will ask the Father, and He will give you
another Counselor to be with you forever—the
Spirit of truth.

JOHN 14:16-17

KEY VERSE

NOVEMBER 30

Jehovah. An Old Testament term meaning "I AM THAT I AM." Used by God Himself, particularly for His relationship to mankind. He is all-sufficient for every need, problem, or circumstance. Every answer is found in Him.

FEBRUARY 2

The original Ghostwriter. God inspired more than 40 writers over a 1500-year period to write down His message for mankind. The words, collectively known as Scripture, did not come from the writers themselves. The Spirit of God used their personalities, skills, and backgrounds (along with a wide range of personal styles). But the message, accuracy, and power is God's own.

NOVEMBER 29

With a correct understanding and relationship with God, everything else falls into place.

FEBRUARY 3

Listen to the apostle John's encouragement: *Dear friends, now we are children of God, and what we will be has not yet been made known. But we know that when he appears, we shall be like him, for we shall see him as he is* (1 John 3:2).

NOVEMBER 28

"To say, 'Of course God is omniscient and knows everything' has no effect on me. I don't care whether God is 'omni' anything. But when I begin to realize that God knows all the deepest possibilities there are in me, knows all the eccentricities of my being, I find the mystery of myself is solved by this besetting God."

OSWALD CHAMBERS

FEBRUARY 4

The "direction toward perfection" process is called sanctification. When something is sanctified, it is set apart for a special purpose. The Christian is set apart from sin for the special purpose of belonging to God.

LEARN THE LINGO

NOVEMBER 27

Changing and benefiting you is only half of God's plan for His Spirit in your life. The other half is changing and benefiting the rest of the world *through you*. A "spiritual gift" is an ability given by the Holy Spirit to a Christian to help and bless others in the family of God.

FEBRUARY 5

If you're frightfully aware of your sins and weakness, there's good news: We will never arrive at the goal of perfection during our earthly life, but over time we can grow closer.

NOVEMBER 26

Are you seeing the big picture? This isn't some 13-inch black-and-white TV version of someone else's life. This is the huge omni-vision, Technicolor, larger-than-life, four-dimensional version of *your* life. How the world will end is all about *you*. God created you. God loves you. God sent Jesus to die for you. God is going to send Jesus again to bring you back to Him.

FEBRUARY 6

Since God is a Spirit, no one has seen God. But God has left us strong evidence—some call it "rational proof"—for His existence.

KEY VERSE

The first recorded word concerning God can be found in the first verse of the first book of the Bible: *In the beginning God created the heavens and the earth* (Genesis 1:1). In this verse we learn two things about God: He created the heavens and the earth; He was there before the beginning of the world.

FEBRUARY 7

Contrary to popular belief, God isn't obsessed with dos and don'ts. So you won't find a huge list of fun things a Christian has to give up. Just the opposite. The Bible teaches that a Christian has great freedom—after all, we're no longer at the mercy of our worst impulses. We can grow and mature in life as God, our Designer, intended for us to do. We can really...get a life!

NOVEMBER 24

The first verse of the Bible doesn't say "*Before* the beginning God created the heavens and the earth." It says "*In* the beginning God created the heavens and the earth." That's right, but think about it: If God created *in* the beginning, that means that God existed *before* the beginning, because in order to make something, you must exist *before* you make it.

FEBRUARY 8

Walk in the Spirit. Allow the Holy Spirit to direct your life. Because the Holy Spirit lives in you if you sincerely desire to submit your will to God's direction, then the Holy Spirit can guide your thoughts and actions.

The Ontological Argument for the existence of God. The very fact that humans have an idea of God points to His existence. Experts agree that a pursuit of, or belief in, the divine can be found among all peoples and tribes of the earth. Since every rational person has thought about God in one way or another, we can reasonably conclude that He exists.

FEBRUARY 9

Was Jesus lying about God? If so, it was a big one. And everything else He said must be questioned. It seems, strange, though that no one ever caught Him in a lie (or even in a sin). Fact is, when the Jewish leaders were trying to have Him convicted, His complete innocence was acknowledged in court 11 times.

NOVEMBER 22

IT'S A MYSTERY

The miracle of starting over is called "regeneration" or being "born again." We are rescued from our evil nature and restored to fellowship with our Creator. Regeneration is accomplished instantly by the Spirit. It creates a new God-sensitive, God-empowered nature in the individual.

FEBRUARY 10

Seriously—while man may bear structural resemblance to other mammals, especially primates, in so many ways man is completely unique. One of a kind. In fact, many people who refuse to acknowledge God as Creator will acknowledge that it requires more "faith" to believe man evolved from primates than it does to believe he is a created being.

NOVEMBER 21

Regeneration doesn't make us perfect. We are still stuck in our human bodies with many of our old weaknesses. Yet we are spiritually empowered to win over the old nature as we choose to follow Christ's pattern for living.

FEBRUARY 11

BIG IDEA

Hell is more than a mere separation from God. R. C. Sproul writes that the problem of the ungodly "will not be separation from God, it will be the presence of God that will torment them. In hell, God will be present in the fullness of His divine wrath. He will be there to exercise His just punishment of the damned. They will know Him as an all-consuming fire."

NOVEMBER 20

"I can see how it might be possible for a man to look down upon the earth and be an atheist, but I cannot conceive how he could look up into the heavens and say there is no God."

ABRAHAM LINCOLN

FEBRUARY 12

God has no beginning and therefore no cause. By definition every *effect* must have a *cause*, but God is not an effect. He has always been and He always will be. God does not require outside support to exist. This is what is meant by *self-existent*.

LEARN THE LINGO

NOVEMBER 19

Reflect on the meaning and impact of Creation for you—personally, because God meant it to be taken that way. We recommend that you read Psalm 19, 24, and 8, in that order. They're brief poems that celebrate God's creative powers. If you read thoughtfully, you might just end up reading the last verse of Psalm 8 out loud: *O Lord, our Lord, how majestic is your name in all the earth!*

FEBRUARY 13

Everyone—not just unbelievers—will be judged by God Himself. As the writer of Hebrews put it, "Man is destined to die once, and after that to face judgment" (Hebrews 9:27). And you can forget about the image of everyone impatiently and nervously standing in some kind of line, like you do at the Department of Motor Vehicles. Once eternity begins, we will lose all sense of time as we know it. We will stand before Almighty God to give an accounting for our life and our decisions.

NOVEMBER 18

BRUCE & STAN SAY

Thinking that he had proved the nonexistence of God, Russian cosmonaut Yuri Gagarin made this statement upon his return from orbiting the earth: "I didn't see any God out there." Think about it, Yuri. When you look at a skyscraper, do you expect to see the architect and contractor standing in the window?

FEBRUARY 14

BIG IDEA

Only God is completely free from all limitation of time.... All spirits, including the human soul, will live forever. But all spirits had a beginning because they were created by God. Only God is infinite in that He is without beginning or end.

Faith requires belief (realization and appreciation) in the truth of the gospel—that Jesus is who He said He was, that the Bible is true, and that Christ is the way of salvation.

FEBRUARY 15

God intentionally reveals Himself to mankind. He makes it possible for us to know Him. But no single word or phrase can express His essential nature. Instead, He is best defined by understanding the many elements of His character.

NOVEMBER 16

Another part of the Holy Spirit's work is to guide believers. "Those who are led by the Spirit of God are sons of God," Paul said (Romans 8:14). Right decisions are determined by right thinking, and the Holy Spirit can be a Christian's personal guide to the truth: *The Spirit of truth...will guide you into all truth* (John 16:13).

FEBRUARY 16

Trust us, Satan's a slippery operator. He knows that the key to "right living" is "right thinking." We won't be "thinking right" if we listen to Satan's rationalizations. Let me point out two simple truths we can learn from the disaster in the Garden: God wants what's best for you, no matter what anyone says; Obedience to Him leads to the best life has to offer.

NOVEMBER 15

No other gods—whatsoever!

The first and second commandments can be violated even if you don't bow or curtsy before a bronze statue. God is interested in our hearts, our devotion, our affection and attention. Whenever we put something else—anything else—before Him, we are "worshiping" another god.

As long as the world and its inhabitants don't acknowledge Jesus as Lord, there will not be a visible kingdom of God. This future kingdom will only be established when Christ returns in glory.

NOVEMBER 14

Satan was a created angel. In fact, he was a high-ranking angel. Because God is incapable of creating anything evil, we know that Satan was created without evil. However, as with the other angels (as with humans), he was given a free will.

FEBRUARY 18

According to scholar Josh McDowell, only God could have created a book of such antiquity which: has been transmitted accurately from the time it was originally written; is correct when it deals with historical people and events; contains no "scientific absurdities"; remains true and relevant to all people for all time.

NOVEMBER 13

Elohim. An Old Testament term meaning "strong one." God is the true God. His strength and majesty reign over all other gods.

FEBRUARY 19

The Mind of Man. The mind, or think ability, of a person is capable of many positive things. But a human's mind is also capable of many negative things.

While humans are "lower" than the angels while on earth, if you become a Christian, you will become a "child of God." At that point, you will have a spiritual inheritance which is greater than anything the angels will ever enjoy. Angels will always remain just a creation of God. When Christ establishes His kingdom on earth Christians will judge and rule over angels.

FEBRUARY 20

The coming of the Antichrist will be linked with another activity of the last days: a falling away or a departing from the faith in the church (1 Timothy 4:1). Jesus warned His disciples about "false christs and false prophets who will appear and perform great signs and miracles to deceive even the elect—if that were possible" (Matthew 24:24).

NOVEMBER 11

God didn't just make the world without being emotionally involved (like, say, a river carving out a canyon). And He didn't make things and then leave (like a kid who makes a sandcastle on the beach, then wanders off). God *loves* what He made. He loves you. He knows you. He will never leave you. And He has an important destiny in mind for you. This powerful message—of a loving, personally involved God—is repeated over and over again in the Bible.

BIG IDEA

FEBRUARY 21

In the Bible the return of Christ is called *parousia,* Greek for the "appearing" or the "coming" of Jesus in glory at the end of the age. The parousia has been a dearly cherished hope through many centuries by Christians facing torture and death.

NOVEMBER 10

A wonderful gift of the Holy Spirit is comfort. Sometimes the New Testament refers to the Holy Spirit by the Greek word *Paraclete* (pronounced somewhat like two track shoes: "pair-of-cleats"). A paraclete is a comforter, an encourager, one who comes alongside. The Spirit is God's way of always being present with the Christian.

FEBRUARY 22

BIG IDEA

Because the Bible is God's personal message to each one of us, it is the ultimate guide to life—and to Him. Besides being a "searching for God" guidebook, you could call the Bible our life instruction manual, written for us by the Creator.

NOVEMBER 9

What is a worldview?

The term worldview describes the way a person tries to understand the world and the way God relates to the world and the people in it. Everyone has a worldview. Even the person who says, "I don't have a worldview" has just stated his worldview.

FEBRUARY 23

No expert knows when Jesus will
return. Not even the angels know.
Only God the Father knows
(Matthew 24:36).

NOVEMBER 8

What about Jesus and the Holy Spirit? Aren't they God, too?

We've arrived at one of the most important truths in the Bible, and it involves a word which doesn't even appear in the Bible. This word, *trinity*, and the meaning it conveys, is vital to the Person of God. Essentially the Trinity describes the three distinct Persons which make up the one true God: Father, Son, and Holy Spirit.

FEBRUARY 24

In reality, whether it was disobedience in a small or large issue doesn't matter. It was still a disobedient act. That means sin, and the consequences of all sins are the same: Sin, in whatever form, violates God's nature and separates us from Him.

It's impossible for something to create itself. Even God cannot make Himself. The idea of self-creation is a classic contradiction in terms. God is what we call *self-existent*. And He is the only such being who has ever lived.

FEBRUARY 25

What do the others believe? Many belief systems do not include the one true God as Creator. Explanations for why we exist and where we came from vary. The inescapable conclusion is that the way we think about God in relation to our existence and our origin shapes our entire *worldview*.

NOVEMBER 6

As a newborn grows older, a family resemblance starts to develop. Maybe it's a big nose, maybe curly hair, maybe a certain way of walking. When you look at the child, you almost see the parent. As a child of God, every Christian wants to bear a family resemblance to the heavenly Father. While that won't include physical traits, it certainly does include the personality qualities and values exhibited by Jesus Christ.

FEBRUARY 26

Our best chance of knowing God is to get to know Jesus, the God-Man.

NOVEMBER 5

Just as you would get to know someone better by first learning his or her name and then by trying to identify certain personality traits, we can get to know God better by learning some of His names (yes, He has more than one!) and by studying His character qualities.

FEBRUARY 27

BIG IDEA

God's celestial checklist has less to do with human time and events than with God's Son, Jesus. Because God loved us, He sent Jesus as a way out of death for those who believe (John 3:16). And at some point in the future, God will send His Son once again to bring an end to the world as we know it. The last detail in God's plan is to put an end to death—the intruder who took humans captive in the Garden of Eden.

NOVEMBER 4

The Holy Spirit Is God. Because the third Person in the Trinity is commonly called the *Holy Spirit* or the *Holy Ghost,* there's a tendency to believe that the Holy Spirit isn't a person or that He doesn't have a personality. Nothing could be further from the truth.

FEBRUARY 28

When the future seems uncertain, I like to remember Jesus' words about Himself: *I am the Alpha and the Omega, the Beginning and the End. To him who is thirsty I will give to drink without cost from the spring of the water of life* (Revelation 21:6). Since in Jesus we know personally the Beginning and the End of all things, we can live confidently.

NOVEMBER 3

God the Father had it in His heart to provide a way for man to be forgiven of sin. God the Father *authored* the plan of salvation. Jesus the Son, while fully God, submitted to the Father's plan. As the sacrifice for man's sin, Jesus Christ *accomplished* the plan of salvation. The Holy Spirit, just as much God as the other two Persons, is at work in the lives of those who've chosen to follow God. The Holy Spirit *applies* the plan of salvation in the lives of believers.

FEBRUARY 29

As a businessman, I always look for the bottom line in any discussion. What does it all boil down to? Here's the bottom line for prophecy: Jesus really is the Beginning and the End of all things here on earth. He was involved in making the earth––and He will return to remake it.

NOVEMBER 2

LEARN THE LINGO

Remember, science is merely a means of observing and learning from what is already there. Much of what people call science is not proven fact at all but theory or hypothesis ("a working conclusion that attempts to account for a set of facts"). These theories can be very persuasive. But theories are constantly being proven and disproven, and what one generation takes as fact can change with new information (the notion that the earth is flat was "fact" for centuries).

MARCH 1

The angels in formation. *Cherubim.* Satan was a cherubim before he rebelled against God. The cherubim guard the holiness of God. They guarded the Tree of Life in the Garden of Eden.

NOVEMBER 1

In the first century A.D., the word *Christian* carried a lot of significance—and danger. Because Christians refused to acknowledge Caesar as a god, they could count on persecution, torture, exile, or death. In the centuries since, the meaning of *Christian* has been greatly watered down. It came to mean you were a white European (versus a dark-skinned Muslim, Oriental, or pagan). These days it can mean simply that you're an American who isn't an atheist.

MARCH 2

King Solomon expressed his frustration with human paradox when he wrote: *I have seen the burden God has laid on men.... He has...set eternity in the hearts of men; yet they cannot fathom what God has done from beginning to end* (Ecclesiastes 3:10-11).

OCTOBER 31

The Holy Spirit never departs from a Christian engaged in sin (John 14:16). In fact, Paul's statement about being God's temple was made to Christians in Corinth who were continuing to live immorally. Paul reminded them that now things had changed—new ownership, new occupant!—and they had every reason to turn away from sexual sins (1 Corinthians 6:19).

MARCH 3

Everybody thinks about the future. It's in our blood. Literally. The eternal God, who made us in His image, built into every human being a desire for the eternal. Some call this the "God-shaped vacuum." We hunger for that which goes beyond us. Yet we're also stuck in the present—limited in our bodies and in our minds as earthly beings. That's in our blood, too.

God doesn't change. He is "immutable"—the same yesterday, today, and tomorrow. And He cannot be changed. Talk about Mr. Dependable! *Every good and perfect gift is from above, coming down from the Father of the heavenly lights, who does not change like shifting shadows* (James 1:17).

MARCH 4

It's time to look forward, beyond our era, toward the horizon of eternity future. Because God is there, too. Just as the world began in a spectacular way, so the world as we know it will end spectacularly. Time will end; eternity will not. Of course, God will be there in sovereign power. But according to the Bible, someone else will be there, too.

OCTOBER 29

If God doesn't change, how come He changes His mind?

God's immutability means that God's nature does not change, nor can He be changed. Yet God *has* changed His mind in certain situations. God is ultimately in control and His will is *determined*, but it is also *dynamic* because of His personal relationship with His children.

MARCH 5

People have tried to discover God in many different ways. For example: *Give God a Test (and See if He Passes).* Also called "putting out a fleece," based on the biblical story of Gideon who tested God with a lamb hide. Your "fleece" could be anything: You tell God if Uncle Harold gets well, you'll believe; if Uncle Harold dies, you won't. Primitive at best. Limited to yes/no replies—and what if God doesn't want to take your silly test?

OCTOBER 28

When is a day a day?

When the Bible says "day"—the Hebrew word used here can have three different meanings—in the context of Creation it is not clear which definition is appropriate. In addition, keep in mind that Moses, who wrote the book of Genesis, also wrote this prayer: *For a thousand years in your sight are like a day that has just gone by* (Psalm 90:4).

MARCH 6

Sin matters to God, because it saddens Him, and because sin brings His children consequences, *and because it separates us from Him;* to man, because we are accountable to God for our actions, and because sin brings consequences, *and because it separates us from Him.*

OCTOBER 27

Day One: *"Let there be light"* (Genesis 1:3).

In Hebrews 11:3 we read that "the universe was formed at God's command." By the power of God's command, "Let there be light," the universe exploded into being. In this dazzling, brilliant burst of pure energy, the entire universe—including our earth, our solar system, and all other solar systems—was created.

MARCH 7

Jesus ascended into heaven. Forty days after the resurrection, Jesus went to a hillside with a group of followers. After some parting encouragement, He started ascending up into the sky until He was out of sight. This is referred to as Christ's "ascension." Even though the disciples seemed surprised at Jesus' disappearance, He was carrying out exactly what He had told them earlier would happen (Acts 1:1-11).

OCTOBER 26

"Being alive to God means that God's Holy Spirit dwells within us to strengthen and develop holiness in us."

JERRY BRIDGES

MARCH 8

The Bible is actually made up of 66 books—39 in the Old Testament, 27 in the New Testament. The subject matter of the anthology includes hundreds of topics, many of them controversial. Yet the authors, who for the most part didn't know each other or live at the same time, wrote in complete harmony with each other.

OCTOBER 25

BIG IDEA

Remember that God had created Adam and Eve with the freedom to choose. He didn't want robots that were forced to respond to His every direction. He took a risk in order to have a relationship with His created beings.

MARCH 9

The apostle Paul tried to put into words this amazing God-Man phenomenon. In just one paragraph of his letter to Christians at Colossae, he used phrases like these to describe Christ: *He is the image of the invisible God, and in him all things hold together, and God was pleased to have all his fullness dwell in him* (Colossians 1:15,17,19).

While it is true that *microevolution within species* occurs—such as giraffes with longer necks multiplying at a greater rate than shorter-necked giraffes because they can reach the abundant food supply higher up in the trees—*macroevolution between the species exists* only as a belief system.

MARCH 10

As the Holy Spirit's power fills us, we become more like Christ in our values and character. These traits are referred to as the "fruit of the Spirit." Paul described these spiritual remodeling signs in Galatians 5:22-23: *But the fruit of the Spirit is love, joy, peace, patience, kindness, goodness, faithfulness, gentleness and self-control.*

OCTOBER 23

God is Omnipresent. He is everywhere. If you are trying to hide from Him, you can't. If you are trying to find Him, He is there. Wherever you are, He is there.

MARCH 11

Jesus had two complete natures at the same time: Fully God and perfect Man at the same time in one person. He was "God-Man."

The box-shattering, life-changing truth about God is *He wants to get personal with every single human being!*

Both young-earth and old-earth creationists (in the debate on when and how the earth was created) date the creation of Adam and Eve at approximately the same time—6,000-10,000 years ago. Interestingly, many modern anthropologists agree with this timetable for the appearance of man as we now know him. A number of them also locate that appearance in the Middle East, close to the traditional location of the Garden of Eden.

OCTOBER 21

Canonicity is the process by which church leaders recognized individual books of the Bible as being inspired by God. The *canon* is the word that describes which books make up the Bible we use today. The word comes from the root word *reed*, which was used as a measuring stick in ancient times. When applied to Scripture, *canon* indicates the measure or the standard used to evaluate which books were *inspired* and which ones weren't.

MARCH 13

Paul said he longed for Christ's appearing, and said that to be with Christ was better than to be alive on earth. *Our citizenship is in heaven. And we eagerly await a Savior from there, the Lord Jesus Christ* (Philippians 3:20).

OCTOBER 20

King David was one of history's most insightful observers of human nature, particularly as he thought about man in relation to God. In Psalm 8, David asks God a moving question: *When I consider your heavens, the work of your fingers, the moon and the stars, which you have set in place, what is man that you are mindful of him, the son of man that you care for him?*

MARCH 14

God's family of believers is often referred to as "the body of Christ." So when we accept Christ as Savior, we are "baptized into the body of Christ" regardless of race, education, or social position. *For we were all baptized by one Spirit into one body—whether Jews or Greeks, slave or free* (1 Corinthians 12:13).

OCTOBER 19

The fact that we can have a personal relationship with this infinite God has to be one of the most amazing truths in the universe! It all comes back to the "loving, personally involved Creator" who presents each of us with an invitation: to know Him; to experience His presence and power; to love Him; to worship and serve Him, and; to receive forgiveness and eternal life from Him.

MARCH 15

Since God is in control, why does He allow evil and Satan?

God is holy, and He will only put up with the rebellious Lucifer—and all rebellious creatures—for so long. Ultimately, Satan is going down to defeat, along with everyone who refuses to accept the saving work of Christ.

OCTOBER 18

God's plan for Christianity involves the church. The word *church* has two meanings: the universal church of all Christians, and a local church of Christians who meet regularly to worship God, study the Bible, and care for each other.

MARCH 16

If Jesus is God as He said He was, then we are confronted with another question, one of eternal significance: How will I respond to the truthful claims—and the personal invitation—of Christ?

OCTOBER 17

Your mind can think about walking, but unless your leg muscles go to work, you aren't going to budge. The same principle applies in walking the Christian life. Want progress? Then expend energy. Just say no to being a spiritual couch potato.

MARCH 17

He's the inside source. The Holy Spirit comes to live inside us. His presence is very real, whether as a "still, small voice" nudging us in God's direction, or as a life-long power to change us to be like Jesus.

OCTOBER 16

LEARN THE LINGO

In the first centuries after Christ, several councils met to determine which books should be included in the canon. Their main task was to evaluate books written during and after the life of Christ. (The Old Testament canon was already settled during New Testament times.)

MARCH 18

Day Six: *"Let the land produce living creatures according to their kinds: livestock, creatures that move along the ground, and wild animals, each according to its kind." Then God said, "Let us make man in our image, in our likeness, and let them rule…over all the earth, and over all the creatures that move along the ground"* (Genesis 1:24-26).

God's final act of Creation produced land animals and the only one of His creatures to bear His very image—man.

OCTOBER 15

We need not be afraid of God. Although the Bible talks about the fear of the Lord, such references usually mean "reverence" and "respect." *Fear the Lord your God and serve him only* (Deuteronomy 6:13). In fact, the Bible encourages us to pursue God and to worship Him.

MARCH 19

As a high-ranking angel, Satan's name was Lucifer (which means "light-bearer"). While one of God's angels, he was an "anointed cherub" who was "full of wisdom, and perfect in beauty." He was considered perfect in the ways he was created. But because of his beauty, he became arrogant and conceited. He considered himself to be greater than God, and plotted to overthrow the heavenly throne.

The big idea of the Trinity has tested the gray matter of great scholars throughout history.... Mystery is part of learning about God. "Tell me how it is that in this room there are three candles and but one light, and I will explain to you the mode of the divine existence," John Wesley.

Walk by Faith: We can trust God for the outcome. Follow His direction, even though you can't see what's up ahead. The Bible says it this way: *For we walk by faith, not by sight* (2 Corinthians 5:7 KJV).

OCTOBER 13

Sometimes Jesus would use an *epigram*—a short, wise statement, sometimes built around a paradox. Consider this unforgettable one: *Whoever finds his life will lose it, and whoever loses his life for my sake will find it* (Matthew 10:39).

MARCH 21

He's the big initiator. The Holy Spirit brings people to the point of decision about their need for salvation and God. This influence, called "conviction," goes beyond an intellectual or emotional power. It is God's Spirit working in the human spirit to lovingly draw us toward God's best for our lives. Jesus said: *When he comes, he will convict the world of guilt in regard to sin and righteousness and judgment* (John 16:8).

OCTOBER 12

We don't know if Adam truly understood what "die" meant, since death was not yet part of earth's experience. God created a perfect world. It truly was paradise. We do know that God gave Adam a very specific command: *Don't touch the tree.* He also was very clear about the consequences.

MARCH 22

LEARN THE LINGO

The Will of Man. Another essential but intangible part of man is his will. This quality usually shows up early in life. Have you ever seen a child with a strong will? For that matter, have you ever seen a full-grown adult with a strong will?

OCTOBER 11

IT'S A MYSTERY

Jesus had to face the inevitable: His death on the cross. Since He was God and knew that He would conquer death, you would think that Jesus wouldn't mind going through the process which would ultimately lead to our salvation. But before His betrayal and arrest, Jesus prayed in great anguish, asking His Father to stop what was about to happen. Yet He ended His prayer with, "Not my will, but yours be done."

MARCH 23

But the counselor, the Holy Spirit, whom
the Father will send in my name, will
teach you all things and will remind
you of everything I have said to you.

JOHN 14:26

KEY VERSE

OCTOBER 10

Tolerance isn't the same thing as agreeing that one way is as good as another. The Bible teaches respect for each other—as in the Golden Rule: "Love your neighbor as yourself." But tolerance of individuals does not mean that spiritual truth should be abandoned, ignored, or watered down.

MARCH 24

God gave Christians power to spread the message of Christ around the world. As the Gospels (Matthew, Mark, Luke, and John) tell the story of Jesus' arrival in our world, so the book of Acts tells the story of the arrival and deeds of the Holy Spirit. When He arrived, the Holy Spirit changed the disciples' lives immediately and dramatically.

OCTOBER 9

BRUCE & STAN SAY

The Bible says that "God so loved the *world*" (meaning all humanity). And He is not willing that *anyone* should perish. In fact, Jesus got a bad reputation with the religious crowd of His day because He spent so much time hanging out with pagans and prostitutes.

MARCH 25

When it comes to the Trinity, we can talk about the "tri-personality" of God. In other words, God has many distinct personality traits, but He also is three unique Persons, each one with individual personality traits.

OCTOBER 8

LEARN THE LINGO

Father. A New Testament term. God is a heavenly Father to those who become His children by faith in His Son, Jesus Christ.

MARCH 26

When you think about what God had in mind when He made the Garden of Eden and a man and woman to live there, what words come to your mind? Perhaps words like *peace, beauty, innocence, perfection.* We think God also had in mind words like *gratitude* and *worship* (man's response to God the Creator).

OCTOBER 7

Let's sort out the views about God and gods with three words: *Monotheism* is the belief that there is but *one* God. *Atheism* is the belief that there is *no* god. *Polytheism* is the belief that there are *many* gods.

LEARN THE LINGO

MARCH 27

The Creation account in Genesis 1 and 2 is not trying to be a scientific log, but it is completely compatible with all that we know scientifically about the beginning of the universe.

Of the major religions of the world, only three are monotheistic: Judaism, Christianity, and Islam. Most primitive religions, including those practiced during Old Testament days, believe in one supreme god, who is the source of all things. But the god of these religions is usually considered unapproachable, so more gods with different purposes are added.

The Holy Spirit gave Jesus special power to begin His public ministry. When Jesus was about 30 years old, He was baptized and received the Holy Spirit.

OCTOBER 5

The Teological Argument for the existence of God. There is order, harmony, purpose, and intelligence in nature and the world. Logic suggests that an intelligent and purposeful being produced it.

MARCH 29

When the Messiah was to be born, the Spirit conceived a miracle. We can't explain how Jesus was conceived in the womb of the virgin Mary, but we know that it was brought about by the Holy Spirit. Can you imagine Mary's thoughts when she heard the Holy Spirit's plan for her!

OCTOBER 4

The good news is that the Holy Spirit isn't just history—part of an exciting early church, but put away in God's closet since then. The Holy Spirit is active everywhere in our world, drawing unbelievers to God and living in Christians with life-changing power.

MARCH 30

KEY VERSE

Perhaps the apostle Peter best summed it up: *For prophecy never had its origin in the will of man, but men spoke from God as they were carried along by the Holy Spirit* (2 Peter 1:21).

OCTOBER 3

The Holy Spirit filled the disciples on the Day of Pentecost. After the resurrection and ascension of Jesus, the disciples were waiting in Jerusalem, as Jesus had instructed. This event is called the "Day of Pentecost." It marks the arrival of the Holy Spirit. The report of the event in Acts 2 says that the disciples immediately began to preach about Jesus Christ in languages they didn't even know.

MARCH 31

God offers His grace freely to mankind. Grace means "unmerited favor." When we speak of God's grace, it means that God offers salvation to us even though we don't deserve it. Salvation is made available to us at great cost to God (the death of Jesus).

OCTOBER 2

As you get to know God better, you fall in love with Him more. As you gain deeper understanding of His holiness, your respect for Him increases. *May the words of my mouth and the meditation of my heart be pleasing in your sight, O Lord, my Rock and my Redeemer* (Psalm 19:14).

APRIL 1

Don't forget, Satan is not the opposite of God. He is not equal to God in power or influence. With God on our side and living in obedience to Him, we can be on the winning side!

OCTOBER 1

BIG IDEA

Remember, God has no equal, and no opposite either. But most of us think of Satan as locked in an even battle with God Himself. Yet the devil isn't even in the same league as God. He's someone dangerous...but not all powerful. Let this important truth encourage you.

APRIL 2

The Holy Spirit brings God as close as possible to us while we are still living here on earth. He didn't want just to be near us. He wanted to be inside us, with us always. Jesus said, *I will ask the Father, and he will give you another Counselor to be with you forever—the Spirit of truth* (John 14:16-17).

SEPTEMBER 30

The Bible was written in three languages: 1. Hebrew (the language of most of the Old Testament), 2. Aramaic (the common language of the Near East for several centuries), and 3. Greek (the international language at the time of Christ). It was written over a span of centuries—about 1500 years, starting with Moses and Job, and ending with the apostle John.

APRIL 3

In the Garden of Eden, where man was perfect, the likeness of man to God must have been even more marked. But even after man disobeyed God, His imprint remained. As God told Noah years later: *Whoever shed the blood of man, by man shall his blood be shed; for in the image of God has God made man* (Genesis 9:6).

SEPTEMBER 29

Just like with the rest of what the Bible has to say, its information about prophecy can be trusted (it comes from God Himself). And the main message to keep in mind about "The End" is this: God is alive; He is coming back to earth; an eternal destiny of heaven or hell awaits us all.

APRIL 4

The Holy Spirit is not just an abstract concept. He is not a vapor, an essence, or a force. The Holy Spirit has existed for eternity with God the Father and Jesus Christ the Son. Like the other members of the Trinity, He is a person. He has a personality. Being a "person" doesn't mean that the Holy Spirit has a body.

Here's how Paul summarized the meaning of Jesus' life: *But God demonstrate his own love for us in this: While we were still sinners, Christ died for us* (Romans 5:8).

You asked Christ to cleanse and change your heart. Why is sin still a problem? As a young Christian—and even as a mature Christian—sin interferes with your close relationship with your heavenly Father. Some days, failure is all you have to show for your effort. As fathers ourselves, we want to tell you something very important: *On those days, open your hands to receive a "grace note" from God.*

GLAD YOU ASKED

SEPTEMBER 27

God is Eternal. He is not defined by time. He always was; He always will be. There was never a time when He did not exist; there will never be a time when He will not exist. *Do you not know? Have you not heard? The Lord is the everlasting God, the Creator of the ends of the earth. He will not grow tired or weary, and his understanding no one can fathom* (Isaiah 40:28).

APRIL 6

Jesus Himself said: *I am the way and the truth and the life. No one comes to the Father except through me* (John 14:6).

SEPTEMBER 26

BIG IDEA

Maybe now you can see how this mysterious, amazing God—who is One, three-in-One, and the *only* One—can impact your life today. Because God chooses to express His fullness completely in those who believe in Him, it's possible for you to become who you were really meant to be!

APRIL 7

We need to qualify what we mean by "man." The Hebrew word for "man" in Genesis 1:27 means "mankind." The Greek equivalent would be "anthropos," from which we get our word anthropology, which is the science of man (you and I are anthropods). So when the Bible or we use the word "man" in this context, it means "humans"—both male and female.

Jesus died by crucifixion. After three years of public ministry as a teacher, healer, and friend, Jesus went to Jerusalem for the last time. Here the real reason for His life became apparent.

APRIL 8

A line from an old hymn says, "This world is not my home, I'm just passing through." Christians eagerly look forward to the return of Christ when His eternal kingdom will be set up. And the closer you get to the end of your earthly walk, the more anticipation you tend to feel.

SEPTEMBER 24

Don't be deceived! Angels and demons are real. Very real. Angels are the agents of God and do His bidding, including defending us. Demons are the agents of Satan, the chief demon, who has declared war on God. Their main target in this war? You.

BIG IDEA

APRIL 9

Walk in Truth. God's Word is definitely the best source for information on His desires for our character and conduct. Jesus prayed to God the Father for the disciples: *Sanctify them by the truth; your word is truth* (John 17:17).

SEPTEMBER 23

God is Love. While God's justice and holiness require a penalty for our sin, His love caused Him to send His Son, Jesus, as a sacrifice for our sins. God's love is not a "romantic feeling" (as Hollywood usually defines *love*). Instead, God's love means unselfishness and commitment. He is ready to forgive, longing to be merciful.

APRIL 10

It is important to know that believing God exists is not enough to get us back into a right relationship with God. The Bible says that even Satan and the demons believe God exists. You could correctly conclude that it is possible to believe in the existence of God and still be separated from Him forever.

Take the great truth of 1 John 4:8, *God is love*. Many people want to think that because God is love, He doesn't punish evil. But remember that God's characteristic of love doesn't operate independently from His other characteristics, including holiness and justice. God's love does not overpower His own holiness.

APRIL 11

These days everyone is looking for a loophole, a shortcut, or a discount. It's only natural that people would look for alternative ways to find spiritual salvation. And in an era when tolerance is revered, it may seem harsh to reject all other ways to God except through Jesus. But according to the Bible, there's only one way of salvation: faith in Jesus Christ.

SEPTEMBER 21

The Bible describes angels and demons as actual creatures—not just illusions, or figments of the imagination, or symbols of good and evil. They have a personal existence and possess qualities of persons: for example, intelligence, emotions, and will. But, like God, they don't have bodies.

APRIL 12

Therefore, if anyone is in Christ, he is a new creation; the old has gone, the new has come.

2 CORINTHIANS 5:17

SEPTEMBER 20

Demons. These are the "bad guy" angels. Satan, the leader, and all of his stooges make up this group. They are sometimes referred to as "unclean spirits" or "evil spirits" in the Bible.

APRIL 13

The Bible does not promise us that the Christian's life will be free of difficulties, but it does promise that the Holy Spirit will be "the Comforter" through those difficulties. God's Spirit reminds us of His power, love, and sovereign control. One important reassurance in hard times is that we are part of God's family and have a wonderful future.

BIG IDEA

SEPTEMBER 19

Mature Christians are usually better at resting peacefully in God's goodness. They agree with Paul: "My God will meet all your needs according to his riches in Christ Jesus" (Philippians 4:19). Veteran walkers draw deeply on the peace of God that Paul says "transcends all understanding" (Philippians 4:7).

APRIL 14

God holds us accountable for the truths we know. But He's never going to sit you down for an essay test on the Trinity.

SEPTEMBER 18

LEARN THE LINGO

The angels in formation. *The Archangel.*
This is the highest-ranking angel. His name is
Michael. At the end of the world, he will lead
the angelic armies of heaven against Satan
and the demons.

APRIL 15

"Faith is living, daring confidence in God's grace, so sure and certain that the believer would stake his life on it a thousand times."

MARTIN LUTHER

SEPTEMBER 17

He will command his angels concerning you to guard you in all your ways; they will lift you up in their hands, so that you will not strike your foot against a stone.

PSALM 91:11-12

APRIL 16

For since the creation of the world God's invisible qualities—his eternal power and divine nature—have been clearly seen, being understood from what has been made, so that men are without excuse (Romans 1:20). What Paul was saying was that creation itself—that which was "made"—clearly points to the Creator, who is God.

SEPTEMBER 16

As we've said, the Bible doesn't present itself as a science manual, but it does give some intriguing clues to the how of the universe's origins. We know from Hebrews 11:3 that God created something out of nothing *by His command.*

APRIL 17

The Moral Argument for the existence of God. One of the characteristics of humans is that we have a moral code—a built-in sense of right and wrong. Even the most hardened criminal understands the difference (even if it's pretty twisted). How could a moral compass—often called "the higher law"—just happen? This sense of right and wrong in the heart of every person is evidence of a moral Creator. (And it stands to reason He cares *a lot* about right and wrong.)

SEPTEMBER 15

Bodies optional. While they do not have physical bodies, angels have taken on the appearance of human form on occasions when appearing to humans. In these cases, they usually appear in male form. Other times they are seen with angelic bodies, sometimes with wings. As you might expect, these servants of God attended to Jesus Christ throughout His life on earth, and will be involved in His second coming.

APRIL 18

Faith starts with belief. Some skeptics of Christianity are of the opinion that faith in Jesus Christ is only for the impressionable, the ignorant, the deluded, the irrational, or the naive. They say that "faith" requires the willful suspension of intelligence. Nothing could be further from the truth.

SEPTEMBER 14

We find great comfort (and astonishment) in knowing that all the Persons of God are focused on restoring our relationship with Him. It's not like Jesus is the nice one, the Father is the stern one, and the Spirit is the mysterious one. Not at all. All three Persons of the Trinity are engaged in the process of bringing man back to God.

APRIL 19

The Holy Spirit, sometimes referred to as the Holy Ghost, is the least understood—and maybe the most controversial—member of the Trinity. But who's surprised? After all, a spirit or a ghost isn't easy to pin down and put under a microscope. The best the Greeks could do was to use the word *pneuma,* meaning "breath" or "wind," for *spirit.*

SEPTEMBER 13

"An angel is a spiritual creature created by God without a body, for the service of Christendom and the Church."

MARTIN LUTHER

APRIL 20

The Heart of Man. In everyday speech, we use the word *heart* in a variety of ways, usually having nothing to do with the actual organ that pumps blood through our bodies. In a very real sense, the heart is the human control center for emotions and deepest desires. In Proverbs, Solomon tells his son, "Above all else, guard your heart, for it is the wellspring of life" (4:23).

Adonai. An Old Testament term meaning
"lord." A term of reverence. Used to show a
master-servant relationship.

Man's faith in God's grace brings salvation.
Man's belief that Jesus Christ paid the penalty
for our sin is all that is required on man's part
for salvation. Once when the apostle Paul was
in jail he was asked by the guard what is
necessary to be saved. Paul's answer:
*Believe in the Lord Jesus, and you will
be saved* (Acts 16:31).

SEPTEMBER 11

GLAD YOU ASKED

Would you rather be an angel than a human?

Sure, the flying around part would be fun, and being in the presence of God on a continual basis is unspeakably better than being on this pain-filled earth. But angels don't have the privilege of becoming Christians.

APRIL 22

Think about it. While it's true that no one except God knows the day or the hour when Jesus will return, you do know that someday you will die. If Jesus doesn't physically come before you die, then the moment you die you will be confronted with one of two things: the awful prospect of hell or the amazing reality of heaven.

SEPTEMBER 10

The person who believes in God has taken a *step* of faith based on a foundation of knowledge, history, nature, and logic. The atheist ("There is no God") and the agnostic ("I'm not sure if there is a God") must take a *leap* of faith to deny all the evidence which points to God.

APRIL 23

Yet to all who received him, to those who believed in his name, he gave the right to become children of God—children born not of natural descent, nor of human decision or a husband's will, but born of God.

JOHN 1:12-13

SEPTEMBER 9

Pray continually; give thanks in all circumstances, for this is God's will for you in Christ Jesus.

1 THESSALONAINS 5:17-18

APRIL 24

The Bible contains many kinds of writings. It's easy to think of the Bible as one long sermon. But actually, most of the Bible is history, poetry, and letters. The word *Bible* never appears in the Bible. The word is derived from the Latin word *biblia,* which means "book."

SEPTEMBER 8

The Bible says that we're engaged in spiritual warfare with Satan and his demons. They are the declared enemies of God, His followers, and everything that is moral, pure, and holy. That's why it's wise to learn enough about these evil spirits so that we can, through God's power, defend ourselves.

BIG IDEA

APRIL 25

You are not saved because you intellectually understand and agree that Jesus Christ is God and is the means of salvation. When the Bible talks about "believing in Jesus," it means more than just intellectual understanding. "Faith" is more than brain knowledge. It requires an attitude of the heart, a commitment of the will.

SEPTEMBER 7

The Holy Spirit persuades us to God's holiness, opening our spiritual eyes to see the truth about Christ's life and death. The Spirit shows us our need to choose to receive Christ's gift of salvation if we want forgiveness and eternal life.

APRIL 26

And what is the benefit of salvation? Well, in a word: *new life.* (Okay, in two words.) The story that began with failure in the Garden of Eden and led to Christ's death on the cross, now ends with the reality of new life for every believer. *New Life Now.* Immediately at the moment of salvation, the new Christian's life is changed.

SEPTEMBER 6

Day Two: *"Let there be an expanse between the waters to separate water from water"* (Genesis 1:6).

On this day God focused on the earth and created the "canopy" which makes our planet special and livable. The earth is the only planet with this canopy, which we know as our atmosphere. Under the canopy, there is water, vital to sustain the life that was to come. Again, the Bible is in harmony with our latest scientific findings, which tell us that the first significant event in the Earth's history was the formation of water and atmosphere.

APRIL 27

While *sin* is inherited, *salvation* is not. Having Christian parents is a wonderful blessing and may expose you to the principles of salvation, but the decision to accept or reject Christ is an individual one.

SEPTEMBER 5

God doesn't require us to prove His existence, or to be intellectually convinced. The only step God *does* require is faith. He wants us to *choose* to believe in Him with our will. In other words, it's not so much what we *know*, but what we *believe*.

APRIL 28

Lord. A New Testament term, *kurios,* meaning "sir." The emphasis is on authority and supremacy.

Put on the full armor of God so that you can take your stand against the devil's schemes. For our struggle is not against flesh and blood, but against the rulers, against the authorities, against the powers of this dark world and against the spiritual forces of evil in the heavenly realms.

EPHESIANS 6:11-12

APRIL 29

He saved us, not because of righteous things
we had done, but because of his mercy.

TITUS 3:5

KEY VERSE

SEPTEMBER 3

As the result of his rebellion, Lucifer was cast out of heaven. Along with him, God exiled from heaven all of the angels who plotted with him. After his exile from heaven Lucifer was called Satan.

APRIL 30

God is Holy. He is righteous. No fault is found in Him. His moral character is without flaw. In the negative context, He has no evil in Him; in the positive context, He is completely pure. In other words, He is wholly holy. *But just as he who called you is holy, so be holy in all you do; for it is written: "Be holy, because I am holy"* (1 Peter 1:15).

SEPTEMBER 2

Science doesn't have to prove the Bible, because science always has been and always will be *changing*, while the Bible always has been and always will be *absolutely true*. The more God allows His creatures to discover and know about His creation, the more we see that the biblical account of how the universe came to be is accurate and in perfect order.

MAY 1

No innocent person will suffer at God's hand. No one will receive a punishment he does not deserve. As Thomas Merton wrote, "Why should anyone be shattered by the thought of hell? It is not compulsory for anyone to go there." All who have accepted the provision of God's Son, Jesus, will enjoy an incredible existence far beyond anything they could ever imagine or deserve. It's called heaven.

SEPTEMBER 1

It seems that most people who sincerely seek God believe that *something* in their life is missing. That doesn't make them losers. In our opinion, those who seek God are wise enough to care about the big things in life and courageous enough to look for the answers.

MAY 2

The angels in formation. *Seraphim.*
This is a position of angels similar to the
cherubim. They are attendants to the
throne of God. Their role includes praising
God. They're described in the Bible as
being six-winged, human-like creatures.

AUGUST 31

The Bible, in the view of believers and unbelievers alike, is considered the most remarkable book the world has ever seen. It is like an old trunk, full of pictures and letters from God (your heavenly Father) to you, someone He loves very much.

MAY 3

Salvation really is simple enough for a five-year-old to understand and respond to. Jesus said it best when His disciples tried to shoo kids away from Him: *Let the little children come to me, and do not hinder them, for the kingdom of God belongs to such as these. I tell you the truth anyone who will not receive the kingdom of God like a little child will never enter it* (Luke 18:16-17).

AUGUST 30

Don't allow yourself to get into situations where you are likely to be tempted to do wrong (the apostle Paul's advice was give the enemy no opportunity—1 Timothy 5:14). A recovering alcoholic knows he can't hang out in a liquor store. In the same way, don't set yourself up for failure.

MAY 4

Day Five: *"Let the water teem with living creatures, and let birds fly above the earth across the expanse of the sky"* (Genesis 1:20).

Science supports that the first creatures existed in the sea and in the air, just as the Bible says. But did they "evolve" from lower life forms? The fact of the matter is that science has always taken a huge leap of "faith" on this issue of linking species (distinct kinds of plants and animals), particularly a lower species (a fern) with a higher species (an eagle). God created all things individually and in perfect order.

AUGUST 29

You, dear children, are from God and...the one who is in you is greater than the one who is in the world.

1 JOHN 4:4

MAY 5

You could call the human quest for God "The Pursuit, Side 1." We try to understand God, to know Him. We have a curiosity about Him. There's also, "The Pursuit, Side 2," God is pursuing *us*. He desires to be understood, to be known, to be trusted. What He wants most is to establish a personal relationship with each human—those one-of-a-kind beings made in His own image.

AUGUST 28

God is the only uncreated (self-existent) being in the universe. All other things past, present, and future had a beginning (even other supernatural powers like angels, demons, and Satan). All things in the universe owe their existence to God.

MAY 6

KEY VERSE

Therefore, if anyone is in Christ, he is a new creation; the old has gone, the new has come.... God made him who had no sin to be sin for us, so that in him we might become the righteousness of God.

2 CORINTHIANS 5:17,21

AUGUST 27

In the beginning God created the heavens and the earth (Genesis 1:1). If you think about it, you'll see how power-packed this simple verse really is. It declares: God exists; Our world had a beginning (it hasn't always been around); God made our world.

God's Holy Spirit is neither male nor female. Yet when the Bible refers to the Holy Spirit with the personal pronoun *he* instead of *it,* we're reminded that the Holy Spirit is a real person.

AUGUST 26

Keep in mind that it is not necessary for us to believe in God in order for Him to exist. God exists whether we believe in Him or not. You see, God isn't just *our idea*. God exists apart from us.

MAY 8

If Jesus isn't God and He wasn't lying, was He a lunatic to claim to be deity? But His behavior in dealing with people doesn't seem crazy. And His teachings (considered to be moral and ethical) certainly do not appear to be the rantings and ravings of a madman. Even by unbelievers, Christ is universally recognized as a great teacher and humanitarian.

AUGUST 25

LEARN THE LINGO

Witnessing (sharing your faith with someone) isn't any more complicated than telling someone you care about how and why you became a Christian, or how you feel about your relationship with God.

MAY 9

BIG IDEA

Recognizing Christ's popularity, religious leaders plotted to put Him to death. After all, Jesus threatened their system of rules and regulations. Jesus taught that what was in the heart mattered most, and that a person's relationship with God was more important than any religious ritual. If the people believed this, then the job security of the religious establishment was in trouble.

AUGUST 24

The early believers who were willing to die for Jesus weren't responding to some kind of divine robot that had performed perfectly. They had witnessed firsthand this God-Man being. He had a name, a face, a human touch. He was Jesus, the Christ—and He had changed their lives.

MAY 10

When the Bible talks about faith and belief, much more is meant than merely confidence in a certain circumstance (such as "I have faith in gravity," or "I believe the sun will rise tomorrow"). The kind of faith which leads to salvation involves attitudes of your mind (belief), your spirit (trust), and your heart (adoration).

AUGUST 23

The most common way to arrive at your worldview [a fancy word that describes the way we understand the world] is through tradition. You believe something because your family's done it or thought it for years. This would be like saying, "I'm a fourth-generation Democrat," or, "My pappy was a Baptist, and my grand-pappy was a Baptist before him—that's why *I'm* a Baptist!"

MAY 11

Listen to Paul's encouragement to the Christians at Rome: *Once the Spirit of him who raised Christ Jesus from the dead lives within you he will, by that same Spirit, bring to your whole being new strength and vitality* (Romans 8:11, PHILLIPS).

AUGUST 22

The canon councils (remember these were the early church leaders who recognized God's inspired Word) followed strict guidelines to determine which books qualified as Scripture. 1. Does it speak with God's authority? 2. Is it written by a man of God speaking to us as a prophet of God? 3. Does it have the authentic stamp of God? 4. Does it impact us with the power of God? 5. Was it accepted by the people of God?

MAY 12

Jesus' life story, which began in eternal splendor, will continue in that way. The life of Christ on earth—when He touched the hurting human race with His own human hands—is only part of the most amazing life story of all.

AUGUST 21

Key point: Remember that the canon councils did not *declare* a book to be from God. They simply *recognized* the authority that was already there.

MAY 13

A high priest in Bible times was the go-between—he made offerings and prayers to God on behalf of a worshiper, and he expressed forgiveness and blessings to the worshiper on behalf of God. But now Christ is our high priest. Paul calls Him the "one mediator between God and men, the man Christ Jesus" (1 Timothy 2:5).

AUGUST 20

Jewish religious teachers often called God "the Incomprehensible One." That's why it's a good thing that God has chosen to tell us who He is. He's accomplished this primarily through His Word, the Bible, through the life and teachings of His Son, Jesus Christ, and through the insight of His Holy Spirit.

IT'S A MYSTERY

MAY 14

You ask us: "If God can do anything, can He make a rock so large that He cannot lift it?" Okay, we're stumped! We admit it.... If you wonder whether God can make 1+1=3, we simply respond that such a question is not about God's power; it's about arithmetic.

AUGUST 19

"What can be more foolish than to think that all this rare fabric of heaven and earth could come by chance, when all the skill of science is not able to make an oyster."

JEREMY TAYLOR

MAY 15

Did Jesus rise from the dead in spirit only?

Gripping accounts in Luke 24 and John 20 show that Christ came back to life in bodily form. It wasn't just a resurrection of His "spirit" or His "essence." When Jesus appeared to the disciples later, His body had all its familiar features, including the marks from the crucifixion (John 29:19-30). He could walk, talk, and eat (Luke 24:13-45).

AUGUST 18

By the way, we're not recommending you choose the Christian point of view simply because it seems more pleasant. That would be using your religious belief as an emotional crutch. Instead, we would ask you to consider the Christian worldview because it is reasonable, right, and true.

MAY 16

God is Omnipotent. He is all-powerful. No person, nation, or confederation, whether of this earth or beyond, can conquer Him. He is able to do anything consistent with His own nature.

AUGUST 17

In Paul's letter to the church in Rome, he encouraged the Christians there to be changed by the truth, not by popular notions. *Do not conform any longer to the pattern of this world, but be transformed by the renewing of your mind* (Romans 12:2).

MAY 17

"Alexander, Caesar, Charlemagne, and I myself have founded great empires. But Jesus alone founded his empire upon love, and to this very day, millions would die for Him. Jesus Christ was more than a man."

NAPOLEON BONAPARTE

AUGUST 16

Faith results in worship. A sure sign of saving faith is the desire to worship God (to "worship" means to adore God, to give Him praise and reverent devotion). This rises naturally from an appreciation for the gift of salvation at the great cost of the sacrificial death of Jesus. A response of gratitude to God flows from true faith.

MAY 18

"Is it possible, not just to have a spiritual experience, but to experience the one true God?" Our answer to the question? Yes. It all goes back to Jesus' first reassurance to His disciples when He told them He was returning to heaven: *I will never leave you. I will send you My Spirit of truth* (John 16:5-16).

AUGUST 15

While many view the Genesis account as superstition, science is anything but exact when it comes to explaining how we got here. In fact, many evolutionary theories are illogical because they have to rely on this absurd proposition: *It is possible for something to come from nothing.*

MAY 19

You might as well add another personality trait to what you're learning about God: jealousy. In a divine, righteous sort of way, God is a jealous God. He says so straight out in the second commandment: *You shall not make for yourself an idol in the form of anything in heaven above or on the earth beneath or in the waters below...for I, the Lord your God, am a jealous God* (Exodus 20:4-5).

AUGUST 14

Here's a Latin phrase philosophers use *Ex nihilo, nihil fit.* It means, "From nothing, nothing comes." Something can't come from nothing on its own power. Therefore, before our universe existed, there had to be something, a "force with intelligence and purpose"—a Creator. Otherwise, there would still be nothing.

MAY 20

Jesus effectively used *questions*. His rhetorical questions were usually mind-benders. For example, "What good will it be for a man if he gains the whole world, yet forfeits his soul? Or what can a man give in exchange for his soul?" (Matthew 16:26).

AUGUST 13

Jesus loved to use *object lessons*, illustrating His point with some nearby item or circumstance. When He noticed a widow contributing to the temple treasury, He took the opportunity to teach His disciples a lesson about sacrificial giving (Luke 21:1-4).

MAY 21

No nation owns God or Christianity in any special way. While in the times of the Old Testament God showed special favor to the Jews, salvation through Jesus Christ is available equally to all mankind. *Here there is no Greek or Jew, circumcised or uncircumcised, barbarian, Scythian, slave or free, but Christ is all, and is in all* (Colossians 3:11).

AUGUST 12

Since God is in control, why does He allow evil and Satan?

God is neither good because He made angels, nor bad because He allows evil. He exists apart from these realities. God is sovereign, which means nothing good or evil happens outside His control. Satan runs free because God allows it, even if we don't understand why.

GLAD YOU ASKED

MAY 22

The Bible has one theme and one message throughout. From Genesis to Revelation, the books of the Bible record one internally consistent point of view about God and man.

Jesus clearly recognized His special powers when He quoted verses from Isaiah and applied them to Himself: *The Spirit of the Lord is on me, because he has anointed me to preach good news to the poor. He has sent me to proclaim freedom for the prisoners and recovery of sight for the blind, to release the oppressed, to proclaim the year of the Lord's favor* (Luke 4:18-19).

When the disciple Thomas refused to believe Jesus had risen from the dead unless he could touch the nail marks, Jesus told him: *Because you have seen me, you have believed; blessed are those who have not seen and yet have believed* (John 20:29). Jesus knew that for an unbelieving heart, no number of miracles would ever be enough.

AUGUST 10

Practically every nation living around Israel in Old Testament times had multiple gods. Throughout history men have tried to get away from a just and holy God by inventing gods of their own. Sometimes these other gods are literal images. They are given names in an organized system. The religion of Hinduism, for example, has thousands of gods.

MAY 24

BRUCE & STAN SAY

What about all the people who *didn't* get healed or raised from the dead? While John says that many things Jesus did aren't recorded, Jesus certainly didn't do as many miracles as His followers wanted. He knew that most wanted the miracles more than the message behind the miracles—that Jesus was God, and that His teachings could change the world.

AUGUST 9

God is a Spirit, which means He usually chooses not to physically write what He's thinking. Yet the Bible says that God *speaks* things into existence: *By faith we understand that the universe was formed at God's command, so that what is seen was not made out of what was visible* (Hebrews 11:3). That's how He wrote the Bible, also called the Word of God.

MAY 25

For the mystery-riddled and brain-weary, maybe now would be a good time to quote that famous agnostic, Mark Twain: "Most people are bothered by those passages in Scripture which they cannot understand. The Scripture which troubles me most is the Scripture I do understand."

There are limitations to God's omnipotence—in two areas: He cannot do things contrary to His nature. For example, He cannot lie and He cannot sin. He has *chosen* not to do certain things. For example, He chose not to spare His Son from death on the cross.

MAY 26

Just because Jesus didn't sin doesn't mean He didn't experience and express emotions. For example, when He saw dishonest money changers doing business in the temple, He was outraged (John 2:13-16). He made a whip out of cords, overturned the tables, dumped all the money on the floor, and drove out the rascals. And it's probably safe to conclude that Jesus wasn't smiling the whole time. Yet He didn't sin.

AUGUST 7

Day Three: *"Let the water under the sky be gathered to one place, and let dry ground appear. Let the land produce vegetation: seed-bearing plants and trees on the land that bear fruit with seed in it, according to their various kinds"* (Genesis 1:9,11).

On this day, God did two things. First, He collected the water on the earth into "seas" so that dry ground, or "land," could appear. Second, God commanded the earth to produce vegetation.

MAY 27

We know that in heaven we will be able to recognize other people (Matthew 8:11), and that we will enjoy rewards for work done on earth (2 Corinthians 5:10). Heaven will be eternally significant because of what will be absent: tears, sorrow, crying, pain, and death. But most significant will be what heaven will include: Jesus Christ.

AUGUST 6

Before God created living creatures, He created vegetation which could then reproduce by means of seeds. Eventually, the vegetation would become a source of food and oxygen.

MAY 28

Rather than think of hell as cruel and unusual punishment, we should remember that it's impossible for God to be cruel. He is completely just and fair: *You are a forgiving God, gracious and compassionate, slow to anger and abounding in love* (Nehemiah 9:17).

AUGUST 5

"Belief" or "faith" that Jesus Christ is the means of our salvation is the prerequisite. We don't have salvation without it. We don't receive God's free gift of grace without it.

MAY 29

BIG IDEA

We walk well when we protect and value our new desire to please God. As Paul advised, "Hate what is evil; cling to what is good" (Romans 12:9).

AUGUST 4

You've heard the refrain, "Blowin' in the wind...." When Jesus was talking to the seeker Nicodemus, that's exactly the word-picture He used to describe the work of the Spirit: *Flesh gives birth to flesh, but the Spirit gives birth to spirit.... The wind blows wherever it pleases. You hear its sound, but you cannot tell where it comes from or where it is going. So it is with everyone born of the Spirit* (John 3:6,8).

MAY 30

Prayer is simply conversing with God. No long-distance calling-card numbers to memorize. You just talk to Him. And you never get a busy signal. Just as in any conversation, you will do some talking and some listening.

Salvation might be the most important theological word you'll come across in this *Guide to God*. Salvation describes how each of us can be "saved"—saved *from* the penalty of our sin, and saved *to* eternal life in God.

Christ didn't give up His godly attributes. He simply took on human attributes as well. In His earthly body, He voluntarily chose not to use all His godly powers. When He was hungry, He didn't turn the stones into bread. But He could have. When He was being nailed to the cross, He didn't call down angels to rescue Him. But He could have. Choosing not to use an ability is different from not having it.

AUGUST 2

Seeking God doesn't stop at salvation.
It's the passion of a lifetime—and will
lead you to the most fulfilling life
possible on this earth.

JUNE 1

BIG IDEA

Philippians 2:6-7 says that Jesus Christ, "being in the very nature God, did not consider equality with God something to be grasped, but made himself nothing, taking the very nature of a servant." Some Bible versions translate the phrase "made himself nothing" to read "emptied himself."

AUGUST 1

If Jesus was a liar, wouldn't the disciples have figured Him out? And if they did, they would have known He was a fraud. The next day—and probably the next minute—they would have gone back to their fishing nets. Instead, they put their hopes, their futures, their lives in His hands.

JUNE 2

KEY VERSE

For we do not have a high priest who is unable to sympathize with our weaknesses, but we have one who has been tempted in every way, just as we are—yet was without sin.

HEBREWS 4:15

JULY 31

What about my good deeds? I'm not a saint, but don't they add up to something?

Yes. They add up to what they are: good attempts. Almost anyone can do good. But with a sin nature, we are incapable of any purely righteous act (Can a fish swim without getting wet?). And we can't add up enough good deeds to erase our sinful nature.

JUNE 3

The Bible says that humans were created "lower" than angels. For example: Angels (and demons) have greater intelligence and strength than humans; Angels (and demons) can move about unencumbered by the laws of nature; Angels can be in the presence of God (while humans can only enjoy this privilege after death).

JULY 30

God is Just. He is fair and impartial. He does not play favorites. *He is the Rock, his works are perfect, and all his ways are just. A faithful God who does no wrong, upright and just is he* (Deuteronomy 32:4).

JUNE 4

The angels in formation. *Governmental Rulers*. Called "rulers," "principalities," "authorities," and "powers," these angels will be involved in ruling the universe later in time.

JULY 29

The rapture of the church is the glorious event when Christ will take His followers up to meet Him in the skies, and from there to heaven to always be with Him. This "family reunion" will include all those since the beginning of time who are dead or alive. Those who are dead will experience "the resurrection"; those who are still alive will experience "the rapture."

JUNE 5

The word *gospel* means "good news." When someone "preaches the gospel," he is explaining the good news of salvation. "The Gospels" refer to the first four books of the New Testament: Matthew, Mark, Luke, and John. These Gospels are eyewitness accounts which tell the story of the good news of Christ's life, death, and resurrection.

JULY 28

IT'S A MYSTERY

During the last hundred years or so, Christians have argued a lot about the rapture. The traditional view has been that the purpose of the rapture is to allow followers of Christ—whether dead or alive—to literally meet Jesus in the air. We would then be a part of His heavenly procession as He comes "on the clouds of the sky, with power and great glory" (Matthew 24:30). Taken as a complete event, this is the spectacular second coming of Christ.

JUNE 6

When you walk across a cow pasture, you have to watch your step. You wouldn't want to have to scrape something off your shoe. We're walking the Christian life in a culture that has a lot of you-know-what lying around. If we want to have a good journey, we have to keep a sharp eye out.

JULY 27

The bottom line is that God created the world simply by the power of His word. And remember, He didn't just create "stuff" (like rocks, water, or gases) by His powerful word. He also created the complex physical processes like gravity and evaporation and reproduction that keep the whole universe working.

BIG IDEA

JUNE 7

In the Creation story, the writer of Genesis describes *how* God made the first man, Adam: *The Lord God formed the man from the dust of the ground and breathed into his nostrils the breath of life, and the man became a living being* (Genesis 2:7).

God the Father Is God. This is kind of an easy one. God is called "the Father" numerous times, including this salutation from the apostle Paul in his letter to the church in Rome: *Grace and peace to you from God our Father and from the Lord Jesus Christ* (Romans 1:7).

Few people take hell seriously. But hell is real, and worse than we could ever imagine. Jesus talked about outer darkness and "eternal punishment." Clearly, Jesus taught that hell is a place of eternal torment and punishment waiting for those who reject His message.

JULY 25

Young-earth creationists (in the debate on when and how the earth was created) believe that God created earth in six literal days and the entire universe is somewhere between 6,000 and 10,000 years old. Young-earth creationists interpret the Hebrew word for "day" as a literal 24-hour period of time.

JUNE 9

The Bible tells us that Jesus was deity (God) and humanity (man) both at the same time. His deity wasn't limited by His humanity, and His humanity wasn't overshadowed by His deity (with the exception that He was sinless).

JULY 24

Whether we know it or not, whether we can define it or not, we all have a worldview. And it is this worldview, or personal belief system, which colors everything we do in one way or another. It determines how we behave, the choices we make, and often how we feel.

JUNE 10

According to Dr. Ross, the probability of any one of the prophecies coming true is less than one in ten. The chances that all 2000 prophecies could have been without error is less than one in 10 to the 2000th power. Since any probability greater than 10 to the 50th power is consider *impossible*, there is only one reasonable explanation for the complete accuracy of the Bible prophecies: God made them, and God fulfilled them.

JULY 23

The Cosmological Argument for the existence of God. Every effect must have a cause. A four-year-old might really believe his muddy footprints "just happin by theirself," but Mom sure doesn't! If the universe had a beginning point—which science also now supports—there must have been some incredibly powerful cause or person to begin it. We believe that someone was God, the "First Cause."

JUNE 11

Dr. Hugh Ross, world-renowned astrophysicist, says that approximately 2000 of the 2500 prophecies which appear in the Bible have been fulfilled to the letter with no errors (the remaining 500 concern events which have not yet occurred).

JULY 22

The unhappy truth about sin is that the seeds of evil in the world seem to be planted in everyone's heart. Most of us have realized at some time or other that the bad-news headlines in the paper could apply to the face we see every morning in the mirror.

JUNE 12

The man without the Spirit does not accept the things that come from the Spirit of God, for they are foolishness to him, and he cannot understand them, because they are spiritually discerned.

1 CORINTHIANS 2:14

JULY 21

The Bible can get a little inconvenient—and might even seem intolerant to those people of other faiths. You see, on the question of "one and only," the Bible isn't open-minded at all. Because that's exactly what God has said. He's it—the One, the Only. *I am the Lord, and there is no other; apart from me there is no God* (Isaiah 45:5).

JUNE 13

"A man who was merely a man and said the sort of things Jesus said would not be a 'great moral teacher.' He would either be a lunatic—on the level of the man who says he is a poached egg—or else he would be the Devil of Hell. You must make a choice. Either this was, and is, the Son of God; or else a madman or something worse."

C. S. LEWIS

JULY 20

We are not on a mystery ride. We're not playing some kind of cosmic hide-and-seek. God *wants* to be discovered by those who sincerely look for Him. As philosopher Francis Schaeffer declared about God: "He is there, and He is not silent."

JUNE 14

Christianity sets itself apart from other religions, not only because of its message, but because of its Messenger—Jesus Christ. In fact, the founder of Christianity made it clear that you can't call yourself a Christian if you like the teachings of this religion (even follow them daily) *but reject the Teacher as God.*

JULY 19

Then God said, "Let us make man in our image, in our likeness, and let them rule over the fish of the sea and the birds of the air, over the livestock, over all the earth, and over all the creatures that move along the ground."

GENESIS 1:26

KEY VERSE

JUNE 15

Just as there are lifestyle choices which are hazardous to you physically (skydiving without a parachute is an example), so there is behavior which hurts your Christian growth. A Christian who wants to grow will try to avoid obvious dangers, as well as "gray areas" that may not damage but don't help either.

God's holiness is displayed by how He treats sin. At the same time, God's goodness is displayed by the pardon He provides for sin. Did we say "pardon"? Yes! You've had the courage to get to the truth about the black cloud of sin. You've endured the deepest gloomies affecting the human race. Now you're ready for the bright ray of hope.

JUNE 16

Day Four:

On this day God transformed the light from the sun into a beneficial energy source, one which would cause plants to grow and produce oxygen—a process we call photosynthesis (remember junior high science?). The Bible doesn't mention these processes of nature by name, but scientists confirm that the order in the Creation account follows the natural order necessary for building a living planet.

JULY 17

No idea is more commonly held by people throughout the world and throughout history than the idea of God—*the Supreme Being, the Creator and Ruler of the universe.* Yet God is more than an idea. He is more than a symbol for good or merely an impersonal "higher power." God is a very real spirit Being who always existed in the past and will always exist in the future.

JUNE 17

Day Four:

"Let there be lights in the expanse of the sky to separate the day from the night, and let them serve as signs to mark the seasons and days and years, and let them be lights in the expanse of the sky to give light on the earth."

GENESIS 1:14-15

JULY 16

IT'S A MYSTERY

God did something very wonderful for Adam. He created woman. *The Lord God said, "It is not good for the man to be alone. I will make a helper suitable for him." So the Lord God caused the man to fall into a deep sleep; and while he was sleeping, he took one of the man's ribs and closed up the place with flesh. Then the Lord God made a woman from the rib he had taken out of the man, and he brought her to the man* (Genesis 2:18,21-22).

JUNE 18

IT'S A MYSTERY

Who is this person called Antichrist? As you would expect from his name, he will lead the rebellion against Christ and His work on earth. According to R. C. Sproul, "anti" can mean "against" or "in place of." The Antichrist is one who not only opposes Christ, but also seeks to take the place of Christ. In a very real sense, there have been many antichrists since Jesus left the earth.

JULY 15

Like any red-blooded male, Adam responded positively to seeing a woman for the first time. But we find no gasp of "Wow!" and no long welcoming speech. Instead, Adam was stunned that she was *an expression of his very being.* Listen to what he said: The man said, *"This is now bone of my bones and flesh of my flesh; she shall be called 'woman,' for she was taken out of man"* (Genesis 2:23).

JUNE 19

The worst person that our world will ever come up with is the Antichrist. Jesus does not mention the Antichrist by name, but in other New Testament passages, this character is mentioned. Paul calls the antichrist the "man of sin" and the "lawless one" (2 Thessalonians 2:1-12). John writes about "the spirit of the antichrist" (1 John 4:3).

LEARN THE LINGO

JULY 14

Not only is faith required to believe in God, faith is also required to not believe in God. If someone says to us, "Prove God exists," we would reply, "Prove that He doesn't." Either way, some degree of faith is required.

BRUCE & STAN SAY

JUNE 20

The Bible is very clear about this point: *For the wages of sin is death* (Romans 6:23). Man is incapable of fixing this situation by his own efforts. But a divine pardon is possible!

JULY 13

Without the power of the Holy Spirit all human efforts, methods, and plans are as futile as attempting to propel a boat by puffing on the sails with our own breath.

JUNE 21

Old-earth creationist (in the debate on when and how the earth was created) believe that the earth and the universe are quite old, perhaps as old as current secular theories propose: anywhere from five to ten billion years. Some old-earth creationists believe that the actual days of Creation are literal 24-hour days, but that there were extended periods of time—sometimes called gaps—between each day.

JULY 12

BIG IDEA

More copies of Bible manuscripts exist
than for any other ancient book (more than
5000 Greek manuscripts of the New
Testament alone). And these copies have
been declared historically reliable by
hundreds of experts in fields ranging from
archaeology to theology.

JUNE 22

Any mental picture we might hold of the invisible, intangible God would be a clumsy sketch of the real thing. Any intellectual understanding we might arrive at of God's true nature would never be more than a beginning. In other words, we can't get there from here.

JULY 11

Just because He didn't sin doesn't mean that He wasn't tempted. Jesus' God nature didn't make Him numb to temptation, but able to withstand the temptations. When Satan confronted Christ with some specially designed temptations, He did not give in (Matthew 4:1-11).

JUNE 23

John wrote in the book of Revelation about his vision of "a great white throne" before which "the dead, great and small" stood before God (Revelation 20:11-12). In one of the most graphic and chilling verses in all of Scripture, John writes: *If anyone's name was not found written in the book of life, he was thrown into the lake of fire* (Revelation 20:15).

Angels. These are spirits which follow God. They are loyal to Him and serve as His agents in the execution of His plan for the world. Sometimes the Bible calls them "elect" angels or "holy" angels.

JUNE 24

Many Jewish leaders in Jesus' time taught that observing religious rituals would earn people good standing with God. But Jesus taught that a person's relationship with God, not his observance of rituals, brings salvation.

JULY 9

The Soul of Man. Heart and soul often go together in music and literature, but there is a distinction between the two. The soul, which is sometimes referred to as the spirit, is the eternal essence of a spirit, the part that never dies. Because the soul is eternal, it is often said that your soul is the real you.

JUNE 25

By his deceptive questions and statements, Satan was attempting to get Eve to disobey God's rules. His logic was slippery. This was the big test: *Would Adam and Eve believe and obey God? Or would they believe Satan's lies?*

JULY 8

The soul is also something which can be lost in the spiritual sense. Jesus talked about forfeiting the eternal soul in exchange for what this temporal world has to offer: *What good will it be for a man if he gains the whole world, yet forfeits his soul? Or what can a man give in exchange for his soul?* (Matthew 16:26). The implication is clear. A soul can be "lost" eternally if a man does not entrust his soul to God. On the other hand, the soul cannot exist without the power of God (Acts 17:28).

JUNE 26

BIG IDEA

We're ready for a working definition of *sin:* Sin is anything which is contrary to God's holy nature. The Bible describes both our *actions* and our *nature* as sin when we rebel against God.

JULY 7

You have probably mastered the art of walking around your house. Hey, you can saunter from point A to point B without stumbling, falling, or injuring yourself or others. But that wasn't the case when you were ten months old. The Bible uses walking to describe the journey of a person's life. Your manner of living is the way you "walk" through life.

JUNE 27

Jesus said that he would return like a thief—*So you also must be ready, because the Son of Man will come at an hour when you do not expect him* (Matthew 24:44). Paul repeats this striking image: *You know very well that the day of the Lord will come like a thief in the night* (1 Thessalonians 5:2).

JULY 6

From the perspective of science, we know that land animals and man appeared after creatures in the sea. Again, science would say that *Homo Sapiens* (the Latin name for the human species) evolved from the lower life forms. Yet little evidence exists to support that theory.

LEARN THE LINGO

JUNE 28

Christ was concerned with the physical needs of those He came in contact with—the poor, the defenseless, the sick. The growing Christian will display compassion in practical, helping ways to people who are unable to help themselves.

JULY 5

In a spiritual sense, the will of man has played a major role since Adam and Eve. God could have created our first parents without the ability to choose, so that they would do only what He had determined they would do. But He didn't. He gave them the power and the freedom to make their own decisions—including the decision that would change the human race forever.

JUNE 29

People have tried to discover God in many different ways. For example: *Look for the Divine in the Natural*. Look for God by studying His handiwork in nature and in the laws of the universe. From platypuses to planets, from bacteria to Brussels sprouts. The fingerprints of God are everywhere. But will you find the Person?

JULY 4

Jesus serves us now as our advocate.
According to the Bible, Christ's ministry
continues today. Not only is Christ alive in
heaven, but He is active on our behalf.

JUNE 30

LEARN THE LINGO

Beyond the Spirit's power to save us is His power for our everyday lives. The apostle Paul knew that the secret to living the way Jesus intends is to allow the Holy Spirit to control our choices and desires. Paul called this surrendering to the Holy Spirit "being filled."

JULY 3

One way to arrive at a worldview is to absorb the ideas and lifestyle you get from the media or those around you. It's easy to do, especially when it comes to fashion, music, and social behavior. But the *best* way to develop a worldview is to investigate the options, consider the evidence, and then make an intelligent choice.

JULY 1

He has showed you, O man, what is good.
And what does the Lord require of you? To
act justly and to love mercy and to walk
humbly with your God.

MICAH 6:8

JULY 2